How to Build an Effective Team

Hiriyappa. B, Ph.D.

Contents

Chapter 1. Introduction of the team
Chapter 2. Management of the team functions
Chapter 3. Team effectiveness
Chapter 4. Understanding the team
Chapter 5. Formation of the group
Chapter 6. Types of groups
Chapter 7. Managing The Effective Teams

CHAPTER 1

INTRODUCTION OF THE TEAM

"Coming together is a beginning. Keeping together is progress. Working together is success".

Henry Ford

INTRODUCTION
The team typically consists of a group of people who are working together with a common goal. Team building is the process of structure, design and buildup of a team for execution of common goals.

A team has identified with its creativity, performance, involvement, ideas generation, progressive development of core competences, uses of innovative tools for the development of a team. The team focuses on creativity, innovative and work spirit of a team member and a team leader. Any kind of organization principally consists of a group of employees, whose main goals are execution of defined short term goals and long term goals. Short term goals are able to perform with the purview of Mission of an organization and long term goals are future oriented and come into the purview of Vision. An organization has clearly defined roles, responsibilities, duties and function of each employee who are performing assigned tasks in an organization. An organization hierarchy divides into the three categories from the point of view of the Management: top level, middle level and low level management. Each level has constituted a team for the execution of planned and unplanned work. Top level typically consists the board of directors and managing director and directors. They are framing the policy for making decisions and administration of an organization for smooth running of business operation.

A glowing team is becoming the asset of an enterprise. The team recognizes the main issues, challenges, core competence, innovation, creativity in the development and discovery of ideas and new ideas through brainstorming; it includes how to manage scarce resources, committed to achieve common tasks, proposes to establish contact with customers, clients, maintain to provide superior quality services and products, and enhanced management skills such as technical, conceptual and human resources management. Team members are taken care of the safeguard interests of the stakeholders of the concerned projects.

Management often focus on team formation, giving training to members and development of core knowledge as well as committed to perform duties, responsibilities as per clients or customer requirements and willing to learn, share complex things, ideas which are associated with the project and able to find gaps which are existed in the projects and able to look for new opportunities such as products, services, customer, clients, core competency in new technology, development and effective utilization of social network platform. These things have helped the team to improve performance and willing to complete a project within a specific duration.

Team building signifies the emergent positive relationships, the ability to learn new technology, interaction, cooperation, generous to working together among the team members in a team. A team offers services to their clients in the form of technical, applications, how to develop business, clients, getting of new customers, finding to a new core system, market intelligence used to make customized research solutions on-site and off-site mode within a specific period.

Team According to The Wisdom of Teams Published by Harvard Business School Press in 1993
"A team is a small number of people with complementary skills who are committed to a common purpose, performance goals, and approach for which they hold themselves mutually accountable".

Team According to MIT Information Services and Technology
"People are working together in a committed way to achieve a common goal or mission. The work is interdependent and team members share responsibility and hold themselves accountable for attaining the results".

Team According Lewis-McClear & Taylor
"A group is one in which members work together intensively to achieve a common group goal".

IMPORTANCE OF TEAM IN A PROJECT
Team failure or success merely depends on the role, behavior, commitment, performance, trust and attitude of the team members in the form of creation, execution plans, finding the gaps in the project, and know how to

overcome the constraints arises during the project, critical evaluation of the project by applying the Program Evaluation and Review Technique and Critical Path Methods.

A team member often involves in self-monitoring, self-evaluating, self-implements and coordinating and interaction with among members in a team.

A team leader has taken all precautions for assigning members in a project: a member must be trained, experienced in the domain area of the project. If the member is a fresher and without knowing the operating functions of a project in this circumstance a team leader would like to train member as per client expectation, then assign to work.

Member can be knowing the role and responsibilities, duties, skills, performance in a project. Team leader selects the members who are quick and eager to learn innovative and technical skills which are useful for solving problems. These things are significantly focused on the strength of a team. Crafts, trained and expertise team members are ensuring the strong pillars of a team and they are willing to commit performance and established an excellent cooperation with others to work on a project.

The team leader is willing to shape up strong commitment of member in a project. It serves the main purpose of the team and make a partnership by reviewing the issues which are critical to the development of members' knowledge. Team leader takes special initiative to find each member's special skills that are acquired from either training or experience.

A team leader specifies and directed the guidelines, rules and regulation to all members. These are related to work, culture, norms, ethics and clearly specifies the authority and responsibility of members.

Management can develop an action plan as well as standard work plan and ensure to move toward sustained team effectiveness and ensure with continued high performance; developing and managing effective teams.

Management facilitates the team in streamlining the process of strategic management by increasing its efficiency and effectiveness in a project.

Building an effective team, is an asset of the organization. It entails consideration of several critical things in an organization. An efficient management has influenced to clients, customers, and competitors by performance, handling the critical problems solving by a team.

Management can know how to handle emotional intelligence in a team and know how to improve individual emotional intelligence by understanding the tendencies which are arising in a team as a whole and learning to manage them effectively.

New teams often avoid the usual confusion of a "team start-up". It is enabling them to solidify more quickly into a focused and unified work group.

Management often maintains a team that is trustworthy, committed to perform tasks, complete the project as per the blueprint and road map of the project.

INTENTION & SCOPE OF A TEAM
Team tasks are independent and multidimensional. It clearly defined by the leader of an enterprise. The Management is responsible to select right team members and specify each team member functions, duties in a team. It clearly defines roles and responsibilities of all members in the team. It's right to identify external customer needs, expectations and requirements in this way to achieve customer satisfaction. It identifies internal customer needs, expectations and requirements in this way to achieve employee satisfaction with the team. Management

encourages to the team and its members to notice ideas, new things how to enhance business growth. It involves complete preliminary feasibility study of projects and its impact and benefits towards to an organization. It is involved in identifying costs, timing and constraints in a team and its project. Team leader identifies the documentation process and method that involved during the time of project process in an organization. Management inspire the team members' spirit and it makes a strong sense of mutual commitment that creates synergy. It leads efficiency and effectiveness in performance of individual members. Management develops a program plan (if the project is a go) or other intended plan to start and will complete a predefined schedule in an organization.

FEATURES OF SUCCESSFUL TEAMS

"Collective work and mutual commitment, in addition to cooperation and coordination, allow teams to succeed'.

Harvard professor Linda A. Hill and co-author Kent Lineback

A successful team is a team, it is involved in an effective team formulating and development: it must clarify the defined goals and mission and objectives. It must identify the needs and requirement of a team and abilities to address constraints in a task and make appropriate plans for able to solve constraints. Recognizing team roles, are significant for achieving the stated objectives.

Management forms a team Charter; it is a document. It is developed by a Management at the time of setting a team. It clarifies team role, responsibilities, direction limitation of team members. A team can utilize individual perspectives, experiences, and skills to solve complex problems, creating new innovative solutions and ideas.

Team members are assets of the company when they are performed performance with hard work, dedication and learn new things and focus on quality, time, and commitment to complete to finish projects as early that specify the team and its members in an organized and planned manner. A team becomes successful because of proper planning, leading and controlling in management and also directed and focused on a particular task that contributed by everyone member of the team. Communicate is an essential component of the winning team. Successful team has to build their own brand identity to get a project, plan project, start project, and finish projects and management of projects in an organization. Team's performance and efforts bring business;

shows on accountability and measurements in terms of quality, quantity, and price in an organization. Teams have become corporate champions when the achievement of a project and getting of a new project. These things influence to get additional project. Management regulate and control the Teams should have to fit into the Organizational rules, regulation and work culture. Teams are ready to handle cross-functional duties and responsibility towards the projects and accomplishment of project tasks and goals within stipulated time. Teams have proper planning for policy formulation, implementation, and control of the project. Teams should estimate the cost and benefit analysis of each projects and measurement of performance in terms of monetary benefits and non-monetary benefits to members, an organization and clients. Management expects proper guidance, suggestion, recommendation comes from members of a team relates about projects that relating to the details and completion of project with cent percent quality. Management instructs to all members who are involved in proper interaction with among the members, clients, customer and the general public. These things are essential to a team. Management ensures the coordination and cooperation among the members in a team and an organization or client. Team and its members are becoming supportive their tasks and responsibilities. The team leader acts as figurehead, leader, liaison, monitor, disseminator, spokesperson, entrepreneur, disturbance handler, resource allocator and negotiator.

BASIC TEAM INSTRUCTIONS

"We must indeed all hang together, or, most assuredly, we shall all hang separately."
Benjamin Franklin

The team is able to determine the meeting with management. Team leader decides who will attend the meeting and who will go to work and mention the member who will take the authorizations towards job in an organization.

Management gives advance notice to team members and project managers for conducting the meeting in an organization.

Management has to maintain meeting minutes or records in an organization and its detail and its approval from team members. Minutes establish ground rules that an essential requirement for the project which is related to the job.

Management notice the changes an agenda in a meeting. Team leader right to evaluate meeting results and focuses on main objectives and tasks in on the organization.

TEAM MEETING RESPONSIBILITIES

The strength of the team is each individual member... The strength of each member is the team."

Coach Phil Jackson - Chicago Bulls

Team members are operating high degree of cooperation and interdependence. It shares authority and responsibility among the members in a team. Members know how to manage, evaluate, monitor and self-control in a team. Team major responsibilities are clarifying the goals and objectives of an organization. Members can participate meeting is mandatory in an organization, management listen all members' views and opinion in a meeting, Summarize all issues in the meeting. Management stay on meeting tasks and objectives and must manage time in meetings and look for consensus decisions from members of an organization. Finally, Management evaluate meeting process in a systematic manner and find reasons for the results. After the meeting, management establishes the proper communication among the team members in a team. Management consults the team and Management makes the final decision. Management gives preference to majority rule or consensus

HOW TO DETERMINE A GOOD TEAM?

An Organization's success is not depending on the vision, marketing of products. It is an effort and efficiency of the team determine the success or failure of a team. A team associated with the right people, who are committed perform tasks as planned, organized and control. Team manager consider of the selecting of the right members to carefully and assess the skills through conducting the test and practical experiments. A member proves their skills that are required to perform tasks and immediately join the work.

The member has clearly and specific to know the roles, responsibilities, duties, qualities as well as interested and highly motivated himself and influence of others.

Team members have worked under the common goal and trust, carefully listening the members' views, opinion. And establish mutual respect.

Members accept the opinions of others and treat it as equally importance and sharing the members each other in a team.

Team members are sharing the information, knowledge about the project and learn quickly that require the project.

Team members take responsibility as well as perform work efficiently and effectively.

Management ensures the flexible work conditions. This brings the effective participating the meeting.

Management encourages the members to discuss and suggest ideas in the meeting.

Management motivate the members for active participation in the meeting and inspire to brainstorming activities. Hence its influence to other members in a team.

Management take necessary steps for safeguarding of the team and welfare of an organization. Management assesses the member's commitment to attain the common objectives; goals, mission and vision of an organization.

Management defines roles and responsibilities; clearly specified nature of work, project and terms and conditions which are related to the job.

Team leader ensures effective decision systems, communication and work procedures; these are very important to the team success.

Management guide, advise the members to keep good personal relationships with among the members and clients of an organization.

Team leader defines the major and minor problems before jumping to solutions.

Team leader encourages new ideas through brainstorming and allow issues concern the conflict and solution of the conflict.

Management introduces the members in a team and provides client details and project details.

Managers and team leaders ensure the formulation of policy, implementation of policy and control project task for accomplishment of goals and objectives of an organization.

A typical team is the collaboration of innovative technology, skills, ideas, performance, committed, trust and common goal of members for accomplishing committed goals.

TEAM BUILDING

It is the process of finding the right members who have strong knowledge in analytical, technical, human, conceptual, leadership, learning and implementing innovative ideas, simplified of the system process, sharing the knowledge to others, enhance team spirit, self-motivation, self-evaluation, self-audit and self-feedback, make and take decisions. Team building process make a team as intellectual asset of an organization.

Management take the responsibility develop a team that produce superiority of customer services and quality products.
Management and members of a team assure the highest customer client, personal and an organization satisfaction and improve the overall function of the business.

CHAPTER 2

MANAGEMENT OF THE TEAM FUNCTIONS

INTRODUCTION

Management knows how to manage the team functions and allocation of resources to the team. Management has responsible to get the assignment from clients and give it team leader. The team leader has responsible for assigning, specific tasks to members and member will make adequate preparation for discharging roles, duties, and functions in a team. Management will take special initiative for the distribution of the required devices, material, experts, and resources. These are required to perform the main tasks and the subtasks of the project. The team leader has right, to allocate and distribute resources to members of a team as per standard plan.

Management provides training and orientation to members of a team. Management and team leader make mandatory for training and orientation for all members. It includes how to utilize scarce resources, development of technical, conceptual and human skills, abilities to perform tasks in a project, arrange fund and equipment, core competency requirement for a project and members who have domain knowledge and experience in a particular task.

Members will know how to the execution of functions of a project. Members are established good rapport and coordination with the clients for the smooth running of the business operation. The team incorporates all activities of a project and will be regulating the complete tasks of a project. A team is worked for a project as a whole, as well as an individual member who is willing to manage and execute team functions.

Coordination is one of the management functions. Members coordinate all the activities in a project with clients, customers, and others. Motivation is another function of the management. Management use this functions to motivate, inspire the members in a team towards the execution and the commitment to perform tasks in a project and able complete the project within the time and budget.

Motivational functions influence the members who are vital the critical and complex tasks, new technical, innovative platform, environment difficulties. These situations, motivational activities such as inspiration, incentives, promotions, monetary and nonmonetary benefits given to members. These things help the members to complete the task. Management will take the care and welfare of the family members of a team who are performing tasks under difficult circumstances.

Performance assessment of a member in a team is another function of the Management. measure the performance in terms of monetary and nonmonetary benefits basis. It is the monitoring and maintenance of ongoing team actions, and make corrective adjustment wherever is necessary and when a member become dysfunctional.

Management takes special care on of systems monitoring in a project. It includes a system arrangement, technology up gradation and makes actions that are directed and the detection of errors in the project and provides training to members know how to operate systems in a client place. Management right to choose modern, appropriate and highly sophisticated technology use in a project.

Management makes a set of procedure for discharging duties in a project. It is manual and it guide to members, clients, customers, and an organization how to operate in client office. Team leader monitors and to ensure compliance as per procedure to perform tasks in a project. It instructs the established performance standards. Management emphasis on team maintenance other than error detection. These activities find the actual performance of tasks than standard performance of a member of a team.

Monitoring and adjustment activities are critically important for an assessment of team performance particularly for teams confronting dynamic and ambiguous situations. Indeed, monitoring activities are most instrumental in the team decision making effectiveness.

Coordination is another function of management. It ensures the effective involvement of members of a team and clients of a project.

Management provides training to all members of a team about how to coordinate with members, client, customers, and an organization. It brings the improvement of an individual member automatically in terms of behavior, attitude patterns these step brings wonderful results in a team because of they perform in highly dynamic and complex conditions in a project.

Management and team leader ensure that the application of these functions in a project is an essence, member of a team need to balance the necessities of project and also finds environment threats: members are willing to contribute efficiency and efficient utilization of resources and act as flexible and dynamic at workplace

Management takes initiative to develop; "regulatory mechanisms" in an organization and it applicable to a team. Regulatory mechanisms include the operating procedures established to govern the activation, occurrence, intensity, and monitoring of team performance functions. These procedures become encoded in a team and new members are socialized to adapt and accept these procedures. Examples of such mechanisms include team performance norms, communication rules, and trained strategies shared by team members about how to accomplish routine team functions.

Creativity and Contribution

Management has identified the team with the creativity of members of a team. Creativity helps the members in terms of update of technological skills as well as advance in technology. The creative team is one which focuses on the application of innovative ideas, concepts and adaption of creativity in a project to perform tasks in a project. Management and Team facilitator encourages the members' who involve on creativity in work, develop ideas, skills, and commitment to work in a team. Management takes responsibility to identify the members' who have contributed creativity in a team and also praise and reward in terms of monetary and nonmonetary benefits given to members.

Management encourages the members to show the team unique talents, knowledge and creativity that helps to the main objectives.

Management permits and exposed the members who have the best approach, suggestion, an alternative method used to solve the problems quickly.

Members contribution helps the organization's success by applying their unique talents, knowledge, and creativity of the members in a project.

Creativity is the output of the Brainstorming discovers new ideas, unique talents, skills, alternative methods. So that Management inspire and motivate the member's involvement in brainstorming activities in a team and it helps the team creativity and contribution

Trust
Management trust the members and trust the performance of the members in a project. A project success depends on trust of the members of a team.
Lack of trust of the members bring the failure in a project. Members cannot show their trust in front of others. Trust is the belief of the members who are working in a team. Management helps the members to develop the trust and interest to perform tasks in a project.

Trust brings the close interaction, transparently work and share the relevant information and exchange the ideas and Information, and committed to working on a project, member's active participation in a meeting and express opinion truly and welcome suggestion from the members.
Management discourages the distrust of the members in a project.
Management allows the members to express their expressions of opinion either agree or disagree are considered divisive or non-supportive. Therefore, Management and team leader maintain the trust who are working in a

project Management encouraged the members to openly express ideas, opinions, disagreements and feelings, Questions.

Management appreciates the members who are learning from the mistakes, and listen and hear other members' voice in a team.

Common Understandings

In a team, members often alert in a team and gives an opinion, suggestions with an understanding of the reality of the situation. A member can understand the game playing may occur and communication traps are set to catch the unwary. Management arranges special training on communication and how to overcome barriers of communication to a team and its members. This step encourages member to practice effective communication. It brings clear, specific, and message can understand each other's point of view. Management has developed set of direction, rules, policy ensures the best communication practice system adopted in an organization. It has established the commitment of members who are given the special shape a meaningful purpose. Management ensures the common understand, it is required among members in a team and frames the interest of an organization, therefore, team members show that the communication skills inherited.

Effective communication helps the members to identify the common understand in terms of the explain team goals, to address team conflict and to build healthy and work an environment, make proper planning and develop the appropriate organizational, technical and conceptual skills.

Management watch the team's performance on the track and will focus on work outcomes. Management gives special training to members who know the sharing process, study the group behavior, strategies for mentoring and coaching, how to guide and instruct properly, how to make issue resolution and to know the strategies for how to bring consensus in group discussion.

Personal Development
Management encourages and creates adequate infrastructure facilities to members of a team. An organization offers special training courses to employees. Management selected the members who have completed the training course as a member of a team. This ensures that selection of right members for the right job. Therefore, Personal development enhances the skills at the workplace and learn at the workplace. Management creates the learning environment for the member who learn and develop the personality.

Personal development of a member in terms of improving communication skills, encourage teamwork, develop motivation and self-confidence, remove barriers and self-doubt. Members must learn skills such as Communication skills, Behavioral skills, Interpersonal skills, Memory skills, Interactive skills, Team building skills, Conflict management skills, Problem-solving skills, Decision-making skills, Analytical skills, Participative skills, Presentation skills, and Innovating skills.

A member bound to develop the personality in the form of an inner self-confidence, develop hobbies and skills which enhance the personal development, practice and learn etiquette and its manners for self-development, smile. It adds more charm and quality on your face member learn and know how to give respect to others and maintain yourself trustworthy.

A member can develop a fluency in communication, it must be Clear and concise communication. a member can practice communication exercises. It is essential for personality development.

Management has set up meditation and yoga practice center in an organization. Meditation and yoga course make it compulsory training unit in corporate training. It reduces stress, anger, anxiety of members and provides lifelong benefits brings the inner peace and its influence on your work.

Development of personality varies from a member to another member. Therefore, the member shall avoid the comparison in the team and be staying amidst optimistic people who are an excellent corporate training tool which helps you stay stress free, and learn Team exercises help you refrain from finding faults, often Be kind and grateful for doing favors and remember who are help you to develop the personality. A member converts Painful endeavors into successful endings and Accept pain to reach success.

Creates and develop your personality by efforts, learn own mistakes from team exercises,

Practice the team exercises. It also helps you to show interest who are in a team, develop qualities such as the sincere, honest, willing to perform tasks, self-discipline, self-monitoring, self-evaluating, self-audit, and know and practice the time management skills and be cooperative.

Conflict Resolution

Conflict is inevitable in a team. Conflict isn't a bad thing, but management encourages the healthy and constructive conflict.

Conflict arises in a team due to disagreement and poor communication of a member of a team. Member can know the conflict circumstances but not know the how to resolve the conflict situation in a team. Management often finds the reasons for conflicts arise the members in a team. Management manages the conflicts and makes an intervention in a crisis situation in a team.

Members realize that conflict is a normal thing for the human being, it arises when finding situations such as an opportunity to find new ideas and creativity in a team. Management work for too resolve conflict quickly and constructively.

Conflict resolution is a steady and continuous process in a team. it will take time, patience and ability to finds reasons.

Management take necessary steps to resolve conflicts arises in a team. It is the responsibility of management try to avoid the conflicts in a team and able to find the issues relating the conflict arises among the members of a team. Management held the meeting and discuss the members about the impact of the conflict towards the team performance, try to bring the amicable settlement in a team. Management notice the resolving the conflicts and maintain a healthy environment in a team.

Management resolving the conflicts by considering the facts, assumptions, beliefs, and decision making without affecting and personal harmful of any members of a team.

Management is ready to resolve the conflict and understand the situation under the individual member point of view and clarify positions, list the facts, assumptions, and beliefs underlying each position and analysis the small groups work on the resolution of conflict.

Management pass necessary order to resolve the conflicts in a team. Management control the conflict and avoid to temptation. Discuss with members, arrange the meeting, send the clear message to resolve the conflicts, and often, insists on honesty and trust of a member view, opinions in a team and do not stick on personal grounds of a member and finally demonstrate respect to all members of a team.

Participative Decision Making
Management encourages the participative decision-making process in a team. It is the extent the team members who allow or encourage other members to share or participate in organizational decision-making. In normal, members may or may not

participate in decisions. It is affecting the team performance and growth. A member participates in decision-making process often brings the positive results. Management takes special initiative for member's participation, involvement in the decision-making process, and monitor, observe, assess the individual member role and responsibilities in a decision making process. Active participation in decision making helps the brainstorming activities of the members of a team. Management curbs the decision-making process of a team when it is affecting the business of an organization. Participate decision making failure to bring consensus decisions in a team. In this case, Management takes appropriate steps and ensure the ethics, code, norms, rules, and regulation of an organization. It helps the members to gain the Job satisfaction, Organizational commitment, Perceived organizational support, Organizational citizenship behavior, Labor-management relations, Job performance and organizational performance, Task productivity, Organizational profits, Employee absenteeism. It involves the identification of problems, providing solutions, selecting solutions, Planning, implementation, and Evaluating results. Participative Management decisions are opened form of management decisions where team members are actively involved in the organization's decision-making process.

Clear Leadership

Management role is identifying the team leader. Clear leadership shows in terms of the subjectivity, self-awareness, and the ability to perceive the relationship among the team members. The team leader must possess the listening skills, communication skills, and negotiation skills, and learn emotional intelligence to manage different personality. The skills of clear leadership are Self-awareness, descriptiveness, curiosity, and Appreciation.

Management tries to avoid the members who tend to work in an unstructured environment with undetermined standards of performance. Management intimate the Leader who tend to lead role, responsibilities, duties and able to the initiative, inspire, motivate, instructs, guidance, to other members of a team. Management and Team leader ensures the develop the structured environment which helps the members who are willing, interest to perform duties and achieved the high standards of performance in assigned tasks and responsibility.

Commitment

Management gives incentives to the member in terms of monetary and nonmonetary who are showing the commitment and do the excellent performance in a team. Commitment brings the excellence, efficiency and personal pride. Management has identified the committed member. This step reduces the Staff turnover. Therefore, Management quickly recognizes individual member services.

TEAM MANAGEMENT

Team management is the direction of a group of individuals that work as a unit in an organization. Effective teams are results-oriented and are committed to project objectives, goals, and strategies of an organization.

CHAPTER 3

TEAM EFFECTIVENESS

INTRODUCTION
Management is willing to bring the team effectiveness in a team. Management shows the special efforts to establish the Team effectiveness. It is the process of selection of the right skill person for the right job in an organization. Management takes the responsibility to appoint the right person and ensure to manage together the different skills individual in a team to achieve particular mission. It influences the team. A team constitute the right mix of skills person such as technical skills, conceptual skills and communication skills. Team effectiveness is directly linked with motivation. It helps the member who has ability to solve the conflicts

without compromising the quality of the task. others factors such as organizational culture, level of autonomy, and feedback mechanisms also influence the effectiveness in a team.

Structural and team process factors also influence to effectiveness of a team. Structural factors include the team, type, size, and composition of skills and abilities.

Team process include the stages of team development, cultural norms, roles cohesiveness, and interpersonal processes such as trust development, facilitation, influence, leadership communication, and conflict resolution.

Team effectiveness considers the performance, task, and objectives of the members in a task.

Teams are blooming in business organization because of their ability to achieve quality results quickly and effectively.

Management is selected the right person for right job who has ready to push to "get the job done," and provide excellence in work in the client organization.

Team achieves the goals of an organization. Management provides an opportunity to share leadership qualities among the team members in a team.

It is involved in effective decision making process in an organization

Management engages the focused discussion about member performance in a team and find the team achieves success, gaining clarity, commitment achieve the team's purpose and partnership with clients brings the productivity that yields better team relationship.

Management considers the Performance of the members and its outcomes. This factor that shape to efficiency of a member in a team. It may be measured in terms of products made, ideas generated, customers served, numbers of defects per thousand items produced, overtime hours, items sold, and customer satisfaction levels.

Management considers Personal outcomes. This factors influence the efficiency of a members in team. It may be measured in terms of employee satisfaction, commitment, and willingness of members to stay on the team. Both outcomes are important for the long-term viability as well as the short-term success of the team.

Performance Needs
Performance and needs bring the team effectiveness in a team. Performance and needs of a members are very important to determine the team effectiveness in an organization: The following list show the characteristics that comprise high-performance teams: members have to build commitment the purpose and make partnership with clients. This helps the members to find the critical issues considers for development aspect in an organization.

Management has to develop guidelines that brings the team productivity by addressing norms for decision making and limits of authority in the team.
Management has to make a collective vision. It identifies a team goals of the next year.

Management take initiative to build an action plan. It has to move toward the sustained team effectiveness.

Management common focus, including the clear and understandable goals, plans, activities, and determine paths to measure success.

Management clearly defines the roles and responsibilities of an individual member in a team.

Management strongly expects tasks as per the defined tasks in the project.

Management instructs, and guide the team how to utilizes the resources in terms of the internal and external resources.

Management assess the value of a members in a team than find the others differences for healthy and productive purpose.
Management right to receive and give each member feedback.

Management collects the details, feedback, comments, favorable argument and also considers unfavorable arguments of the members in a meeting in a team.

Management fix the team goals and measure the goals and find the gaps in the goals.

APPLICATION
Management brings the team effectiveness by application of the significant things in an organization.
Management get the application from team and its members. It is relating a project to find areas of critical do performance.

Management ensure the mission and vision. It helps to team make continued high performance in an organization.

Management tries to avoid the usual confusion of a "team start-up". It is enabling more quickly and get into the focused on unified work in a group.

FACILITATION
Management arranges the facilitation. It is one of the major keys and ensure towards the team and its effectiveness in an organization:

Management helps the Team leaders who are in the critical situation. Management assigns roles to managers who are in charge of functional departments who have evolved into functional and cross-functional teams. Team and its members are willing to achieve the planned performance in an organization.

Management arranges the training the team leader about how to practice, assess, and how get the feedback, learn the skills such as technical, human and conceptual and communication skills. These skills help the members to discharge duties effectively and maximize a team's energy, thinking capabilities and resources. These steps empower the teams move forward the issues, solve problems, and make decisions.

Teams are playing the significant role of the today's business world. Management can be restructured work of the groups. This is needed for all kinds of organizations. Management can understand the needs of the group, behavior, and attitude concept of the group in an organization. This helps the team member in order to appreciate and the individual functions work in organizations and to know the how group can be function in the organization and outside the organization. A member can influence the group activities and behavior of the individual member also influence the group and develop the teamwork in an organization. Management examines the basic characteristics of group, including the types of work groups, the development of informal groups, and to know the operate of the business.

KEY AREAS OF TEAM EFFECTIVENESS

Management has identified the key areas of the team effectiveness. It focusses the continuity of the improve team members' effectiveness. Team effectiveness key areas as outlined:

Goals

Roles

Procedures

Relationships

And Leadership
Periodic Self-evaluation
Effective use of Resources
Control procedures
Self-Awareness
Development of trust in a team

Goals
Management clearly defines Goals, Vision, Mission, Values of the team and frame plans to manage team activities in an organization. Team contribution plays a significant role in developing and achieving goals of the team.

Roles
Management defines the Clear Roles and Responsibilities, Organization Structure of the team, Job Description of members. Accountabilities of team members, Competencies among the Resources, require Tools and Equipment for a team members and have technical Qualifications helps the member for effectively running team work.

Belbin defines nine team roles are outlined:
Creative Team Roles: Plant and Resource Investigator Leadership Roles: Shaper, Implementer and Coordinator Miscellaneous Roles: Specialist, Monitor/Evaluator, Completer-Finisher and Team Worker

Plant: creative, imaginative, unorthodox, solves difficult problems

Resource Investigator: extrovert, enthusiastic, communicative, explores opportunities, develops contacts

Shaper: challenging, dynamic, thrives on pressure, has the drive and courage to overcome obstacles.

Implementer: disciplined, reliable, conservative and efficient, turns an idea into practical action

Coordinator: mature, confident, a good chairperson, clarifies goals, promotes decision-making, delegates well

Specialist: single-minded, self-starting, dedicated, provides knowledge and skills in rare supply Monitor/Evaluator: sober, strategic and discerning, sees all options, judges accurately

Completer/Finisher: Painstaking, conscientious, anxious, searches out errors and omissions

Team worker: cooperative, mild, perceptive and diplomatic, listens, builds, and averts friction

Procedures

It is the responsibility of the management to define procedures for functional activities of a team. It helps the member to find work environment of a team and its member. It is the methods help the member to perform team task in an organizational project. Management uses the procedures for solving problems in a team, and Making Effective Decisions, Communicating, Managing Conflict, Completing Tasks, Planning, Meetings, Managing Change, and Evaluating Performance.

Relationships
Management often develop Positive relationships. It helps the team to develop the team effectiveness. This step helps the team to be the achievement of a team goals. A team maintain positive relationships, Mutual respect and trust among team members. Management determine the effectiveness of the team in terms of the Support, Inclusion, Involvement, Value diversity, Listening, and make effective feedback and give mutual responsibility at the time of disagreement. These things are making the team effectiveness that help the member achieve the goals.

Leadership
Management creates leader for a team. A member is leader who leads the team in an organization. Leader who gain support of all

members and achieve the goals effective. A strong team leaders who possess the qualities as Personal Credibility, Strategic Focus, Clear Expectations, Clear Communication, Engagement and Involvement, Develop People and Team, All members have responsible and accountable, Manage Change Recognition and effective team often aware of the responsibilities of the work at competitive environment.

REASONS FOR TEAM INEFFECTIVENESS

Absence of Trust

This is happened when the members are reluctant and vulnerable with members who are unwilling to admit their mistakes, weaknesses, or need for help. absence of trust demolishes the comfort level among team members, a foundation of trust is not possible.

Fear of Conflict

Absence of trust are incapable of engaging in unfiltered, passionate debate and key issues. It creates situations where team conflict can easily turn into veiled discussions and back channel comments. In a work place, team member do not openly express their opinions, and inferior decisions result.

Lack of Commitment
Management try to avoid the lack of commitment of the members in the team. Conflict arises in a team due to members commit to take decisions. Many time, without conflict to take decision, although it is difficult for team members to commit the decisions and fostering an environment where ambiguity prevails. There is lack of direction and commitment make the members disgruntled and disenfranchised.

Avoidance of Accountability
A team does not commit the clear plan of action. It finds that the management and focused on driven individuals who are trying to avoidance of accountability. Management hesitant to call the members in a team and instruct the peers actions and behaviors. It brings the counterproductive the team and overall good for a team.

Inattention to Results
Management brings the attention the results of the team. Team members, naturally focus on own needs (e.g., ego, career development, recognition, and so on) ahead of the collective goals of the team. Individuals not held accountable. If a team has neglected the need for achievement. It results that the business ultimately suffers.

Lack of Productivity, Wasted Effort and Inefficiency

Team become an inefficient at work place. It results that lack of productivity, wasted effort and have been generated the inefficiency in a team work.

Misalignment to A Company's Strategy and Priorities; And A Poor Dynamic with Ineffective Communication or Mistrust

The team work as per plan and priorities. the team is not set priorities at work place due to ineffective communication and mistrust among the team members in a team.

CHAPTER 4

UNDERSTANDING THE TEAM DYNAMICS

INTRODUCTION

Team dynamics is the process of developing group cohesiveness, problem solving skills, encourage collaboration and make creativity in a team. It has happened in a team and its members. Management find the unseen forces that existed the team. The team consists of the group of members who are having different skills, knowledge, innovative technology used and execution of the tasks in an organization. Management understand the member attitude, behavior, these are changing from a member to another member in a team and to know how to interact member in a team, public and clients. Management can understand the team dynamics in the form of generalizing ideas, creating ideas, planning ideas, implementing performance, resolving conflicts of power, resolving conflicts and interest and ready to adapt changes in a team, a project and in a task. Management has strongly understood the influence of a team and a team about how reacts, behaves or performs, and show the effects of a member in a team. understanding the team dynamics often very complex to management. Team Dynamics of the members are unseen forces that operate in a team between different members of the team. For example, a small team, it consists of six members, in a team, two members who have a particularly strong friendship. This is recognized in terms of personality styles of a member, member roles in on a project, office working conditions, tools and technology are utilized by a member in a team work, organization culture, process and methodologies are adopted in a team for solve problems in a work. Management can understand the team dynamics components such as size, objectives, status, roles, norms and cohesiveness and status of a team.

IMPORTANCE OF TEAM DYNAMICS

Management inspire, motivate the successful Teams and give direction to a team about the clear sense of the vision and mission. Team leader select the right people for the right place and arrange the facilitates resources.

Formal and informal work teams are important to consider competitive factors for survival of the organizations due to changes in organization.

Teamwork become a success. It is the result of members who are working together effectively and efficiently achieving the organizational tasks, vision and mission.

Formal team include the command and task team in an organization. Informal groups include the interest and friendship in members in a team.

The group dynamics benefit the organization in the form of analysis of team systems that use inputs and engage in various processes or transformations, and produce outcomes in an organization.

Management is willing to help the team and able to bring the higher performance from the formal members in a team by assigning the roles to members who assign to particular team.

Members in a team bound to have relevant areas of expertise and have appropriate interpersonal skills for the accomplishment of tasks.

Team dynamics is a degree of diversity among the members in a team that usually adds to performance of the project.

Management arrange training for members who are in a team, particularly for diverse members in a team. This is to be useful and helpful to other members in a team.

Members in a team who may be attracted the other member in a team. There are number of reasons such as liking other members in the team, liking the activities of the in a team, the goals or purposes of the team, the team satisfies an individual's need for affiliation, and the team can help an individual member who achieve a goal outside the team. In the case of the absence of attraction, it can prevent the team from achieving the high performance in an organization.

Member roles in a team such as team task roles, team maintenance roles, and self-performance roles.

The size of the team has also played the significant role in improving the team's performance.

In the case of the Mid-sized team's, it consists of five to seven members in a team that seem to be an optimum size of an organization.

In the case of the Smaller teams can often intensify individual differences in team work.

In the case of the large team's which tend to be working in team's than working alone. Management Provide free riding particularly members who exhibit the individualism rather than the collectivism.

Management find the team who are in social loafing in a team. Management can combat social loafing by several methods such as assign few extra people to do the work, this is the key method to achieve tasks in a team.

Management measure the member's performance in a team in form of visible the performance of individual member, get feedback and provides incentives, rewards to members as per performance and roles, responsibilities in a team. These methods used by management and enhance the performance of team.

TEAM SYNERGY

The term 'Synergy' derived from the Greek word synergia, which meaning joint work and cooperative action. It means working together in a team and accomplish tasks. Synergy also known as synergism. It refers to the combined effects that produced by two or more parts, elements or individuals.

Performance of a team is dependent on the performance of members in a team in an organization. Many times, team performance is low due to the negligence of the team and its members and Many times, performance is high due to planned, organized and controlled effort of the team and its members. This process is called synergy. In another word synergy means that teamwork will have to produce the better result than individual member who are working together team and achieve goal individually.

Member who are involved working in a team, they are able to produce standard outputs other than actual produced. So that, individual member who perform tasks separately in an organization. This is help for assessment of the individual members by Management.

Positive synergy is the force that results the combined gains from team interaction (as opposed to individuals operating alone) are greater than team process losses.

Positive synergy is resulting the group decisions which may well include the generation of more ideas, more creative solutions, increased acceptance of the decision by team members, and increased opportunity for the expression of diverse opinions. Management held discussion of the current interest facts with the team and team building is an effort to achieve positive synergy through the combined efforts of team members.

Positive synergy is sometimes called as the 2 + 2 = 5 effects. Operating independently, each subsystem can produce two units of output. However, by combining their efforts and working together effectively, the two subsystems can produce five units of output.

Negative synergy is the force that results team process losses are greater than any gains achieved the combining the forces of group members. Negative synergy can be called the 2 + 2 = 3 effect. Again, individuals operating alone can each produce two units of output. However, with negative synergy, the combination of their efforts results in less output than what they would have achieved if they worked alone. Negative synergy can result the inefficient committees, business units that lack strategic fit, and from other poorly functioning joint efforts.

SYNERGY LEVELS
There are three key characteristics of the Team that determine the synergy levels. These are listed below:
Team norms
Team cohesiveness
Team development

TEAM NORMS
It refers to the standards (degrees of acceptability and unacceptability) for the code conduct applicable in a team that help individuals who judge what is right, good or bad in a given social setting. Norms are rules or behavioral models that are established by Management and accepted by individuals who belongs to the same culture, group or employee of an organization. It reflects the team's values; they outline:

It defines the nature of the interpersonal relations promoted among members or with non-members;

It determines the skills required by a member in order to accomplish specific tasks in the team;

It establishes acceptable and unacceptable behavior of the members in the team.

To find out the norms of the team has been adopted, it is important to find questions about its core values, conduct and practices.

Management defines the punishment and reward system applied to all employees in an organization. It may be the good indication of the norms applicable by a particular team.

Team's norms are culturally derived and vary from one culture to another. It notices by the management of an organization.

Team's norms are usually written and unwritten, Therefore, it is a strong influence on the individual behavior.

Team norms may go above and beyond formal rules and written policies which are practices in a team.

Norms are rules and code of the conduct which are closwly associated with the behaviors of a members in a team that are acceptable the team

Norms stem of an organization that explicit statements followed by supervisors and coworkers. It notices that the critical events in a team's history, primacy, and behaviors of an individual member

Work team norms are related the performance, appearance, social measurement and allocation of resources in an organization and its approved by the management of an organisation.

PERFORMANCE NORMS
It refers to the meausement of dedicated effort has doneby all the employees in an organization. Managemnt define the standard performance norms that apply to all members and assess the performance of a members in a team and how member can work and identify the contribution of a member in a team in an organization.

Appearance Norms
It refers to the instructions on the appropriate dress code wear by an individual member in a team and its members in an organization. Management decide and determine the nature of appearance suitable for the work environment who executives and different rank of employees in an organization.

Social Arrangement Norms
It refers to the informal work of an individual members in at team. Management prescribe

the social arrangement norms that is useful to be regulating the social interaction in a team in an organization.

Allocation of Resources Norms
It refers to the resource allocation in the organization. It is decided by the management in terms of pay, assignment of jobs and allocation of new tools and equipment for a team. These utilized by members of a team in an organization.

Reasons for Groups Enforce Norms
It helps to the facilitate the survival in a team. This is notice by management It is the simplify or clarify role and expectations of a member in a team.

This is the help members and try to avoid embarrassing situations in a team.

This norm expresses the key values of a team and enhance the team's unique identity.

TEAM COHESIVENESS
Cohesion is the involvement of members who are to be commitment of the task and make interpersonal attraction in a team. It brings team become unity and has committed to work to achieve the set goals. It includes multidimensional skills, emotional needs, group team attractions, team prides, and commitment of the task. A formal definition of group cohesiveness is, " the resultant of all

the forces acting on members to remain in the team." Attendance and punctuality are easy ways of measuring the cohesiveness of a team.

Benefits arise from team cohesiveness in the form of effective communication among the team members, positive instructions to another member. Members accomplish the main task which specify by management, it results the team that becomes satisfied with the action of work.
It refers to the consequences a team communication, satisfaction, performance, hostility and aggression toward other teams, and a team's is willingness to innovate and change.

The amount of cohesiveness influencing the team in the form of members share the attitudes and values, find the amount of severity threats arises the team from external work environment.

This is involved in sharing the team experiences in terms of recognizable successes, the degree of difficulty encountered in joining the team, and the size of the team.

FACTORS INFLUENCING TEAMCOHESIVENESS
Group cohesiveness influencing factors are the Group size, degree of dependency, physical distances, time spent together,

severity of initiation, cooperation, threat history of past successes. These factors are influencing the team cohesiveness in an organization.

Team size
Small group size is the greater probability of being cohesive than large teams in an organization. Management find reasons, When team member size increases. It brings the possibility of agreement towards the common goal and mutual interaction decreases. When team increases, it restricts inter team and intra team communication and encourages for the formation of sub teams.

Degree of Dependency
It is a positive relationship between the degree of cohesiveness and dependency in an organization. It requires greater attractiveness towards goals in an organization. The greater the degree of dependency which will be greater attraction and consequently the higher group cohesiveness in an organization.

Physical Distance
Management maintains physical distance among the members in an organization. It helps to individual member who are working together the near distance. It creates a greater opportunity among the members who are involved in interaction in an organization.

It helps the members in a team in terms of the free exchange of ideas, sharing the problems and prospects in an organization. Therefore, it develops a closeness among the team members who are leading the greater cohesiveness.

Time spent Together
Management spends time together team leader and clients. It helps to bring together cohesiveness. It is positive to members who are related members who have to meet frequently and spend time together for developing mutual attraction and interpersonal interaction.

Management and team leader encourages the developing friendship and communication among members in an organization.

Severity of Initiation
Management try to be correlated with the cohesiveness, and specify the strict admission procedures for entry into group. It generates severity of initiation the member who will to work in a team.

This indicates the team becomes unique and elite in the eyes of member in other teams in an organization.

It arises the natural tendency of the human. It can share among the team members and get benefits who are put their efforts in an organization.

Cooperation
Management develops cooperation among the employees who are working in an organization. It brings the team spirit; this is developed by the members in a team. It helps to members who shares personal opinion, suggestion, and recommendation relating to the team tasks, reward system in a team and teamwork. Management designed organization structure. It promotes the greater cooperation among the members.

Status
Management creates the position. Position brings the status who hold the position. Position gives authority to member and who able to discharge roles, functions, and duties. Status and cohesiveness are positively related in an organization. Status is identity of team and its members, tasks in an organization. Individual member gains a Status by strong dedication, achievement, growth and development of the organization.

Threat
Management often finds threat from the members, clients, and external environment.

Management considers determining factors of cohesiveness such as external factors and internal factors. Management unable to predict External threats and it is uncontrollable. Management able to predict Internal threats and controllable, Its impact on the team, identity, and process in an organization. Strong and united team avoid and tackle the treats to an organization.

History of Past Successes
Past history has been influencing the group cohesiveness in an organization in terms of Past result, performance, growth and development. These are the step stone of an organization and these helps the management to frame the future goals, mission and vision of an organization. Management evaluates the past results, analysis and interpret and estimate the future result for survival, growth and development of an organization.

CHAPTER 5

FORMATION OF THE GROUP

INTRODUCTION
Making of group is a process of selection of team members and train them quality members and aim to learn innovative, technical, conceptual skills and able to manage complex project by applying the skills, talents use for coordinating and interact among the members and clients. Group work as per the instructions, guidance of the management.

Management take responsibility to make group. It brings that the performance of the members of the group increased and expects the best result from the existed group. Management identifies the skills and find gaps in skills, and able to develop skills and gives training to members who are requiring the skills such as communication and leadership skills. Management make the group become cooperative and interactive among the members in the group. It ensures the growth, development, and make members as efficient leader who become to commit the task that assigned by a Management.

Management Facilitates and develops the communication. These facilitates help to members who become show positive attitude and response. This brings the group spirit. Members are self-motivate, setting the goals themselves. Management identify the strengths, weakness, opportunity, and treats of individual members and give coaching to members how to manage weakness and treats in a group.

The Group become successful when the management facilitate the infrastructure facilities and selects the right member for the right job. Management define the individual member roles, duties, function and responsibilities in a project and given the training to member and who become self-defendant leader in a project.

Management identify the members in a group who are become the leader of the team. Therefore, Management arranges training on how to build group. Group building process bring the changes in a team. This process encourages the members who build the good rapport as among the members in a group. It focusses on the ideas development, implementation and control the task of the project. Efficient Group building the brings the efficiency and effectiveness in work.

The group's success depends on individual member's ability, trust, guidance, managing roles, responsibilities, assist and accept assistance from other colleagues. The group success or failure depends on the performance, participation, behavior, attitude and perceptions of the members in a group.

FIVE STAGES FOR DEVELOPING GROUPS MODEL
Bruce W. Tuckman developed the Five Stages for Developing Groups Model Five stages are "forming", "norming", "storming", "producing" and "ending".

HOW TO FORM GROUP'S

Forming
Storming
Norming
Performing
Adjourning
These are five stages helps the management for development or formation of the group's:

Stage 1: Forming
It involves the following activities:

Management considers the Forming stage. This stage helps the management to finds group members and attempt to assess the ground rules applicable to particular task and interaction with the team. This stage determines, define team, individual member roles in a group.

In this stage, Management establish and develop trust, mutual communication. It helps the group and it is defined the task and problems. Management find the best strategy, that identify the information which is needed for forming of the group. Management defines the norms, rules, code conduct task for a member in the group. Management encourage the members in terms of development of the communication skills, how to handle conflict situations in workplace, help each other, how to maintain records, provides training, train for how to make correspondence and how to discharge duties and functions in the group.

Stage 2: Storming

Storming is the second stage of forming the group in an organization. Management identify the growing group challenges, problems, how to tackle problems, to find solutions, plan and alternative plans and changes. During the Storming stage, Members of the group have to do certain activities as follows:

Members realize that the task of the project is more difficult than they imagined; member's attitude, behavior perceptions and have fluctuations brings the success; Members maintain resistant in the task and able to maintain collaboration.

Storming Diagnosis the following activities for formation of the group. common goals and objectives, roles and responsibilities, task, communication, and decision systems work, interpersonal skills,

Negotiating Conflict in the group as follows:

Management find the issues for problems and who creates problems in an organization.

Management look the needs, goals of an individual member.

Management address the problems, challenges, and opportunity and State the members' views in clear non-judgmental language. It clarifies the core issues in an organization.

It listens carefully of individual member perspective. It checks the core issues, problems in an organization.

Stage 3: Norming

Norming is the 3rd stage for formation of group in an organization. Normally, Norming occurs as group members begin to build group cohesion, as well as develop a

consensus about norms applicable to members for performing activities are relating to one another. in this stage, members accept the following issues in a group:
members in a team, rules and procedures; roles in the team; and, The individuality of the fellow members.

Team members realize about the behavior and roles in an organization members develop competitive relationships and become more cooperative.

There is a willingness to confront issues and solve problems.

Members ability to express criticism constructively.
Management creates work spirit among the members in a group.

Stage 4: Performing
In this stage, members are performing the task with support of the members in the group. It determines the performance of an individual members who are in the task. It provides on opportunity to members to the better understanding of strengths and weaknesses in a group. Management ability to prevent and avoid the conflict among the members and avoid the individual difference and able to solve the problem. it brings the

close friendship, relationship among the members in the group.

Stage 5: Adjourning
Adjourning shows that the members of the group prepare for disengagement when group successfully completion of it's the goals.
In this stage, many issues are as follows: Members commitment, helps the success of the group and this help for achieve for goals and objectives.
Defines the roles, responsibilities of the members in the group. Members use the best skills for accomplishment of the goals.

Member participation helps the organization. It brings to develop new ideas and find solution for problems in all areas of an organization.

Member participative the Effective information management systems and processes in an organization.

Management develop the excellent communication system interaction skills for members.

Defines the member's behavior in group and - decision procedures and ground rules in work environment.

Establish the Balanced participation in decisions of the group.

Member know and awareness of the group process in an organization
Maintain the good personal relationships among the members in an organization.

CHAPTER 6

TYPES OF GROUPS

INTRODUCTION
In an organization, there are different types of group are working. Different types of group are formulated due to the need and requirement of the work of an organization.

TYPES OF GROUP
Informal group
Reference group
Small group
Friendship group
Task group
Formal group
Self-managed group
Self-directed group
Virtual group

Informal Group

It refers to a collection of people seeking friendship and acceptance that satisfies esteem needs.

It refers the members who belong to various divisions or sections irrespective of their jobs. These groups are formed for solving any serious problems in an organization.

Formal Group

It refers to the collection of people who have created to do something productive that contributes to the success of the larger organization. It can form line authority in a group

These groups are formed for a specific purpose in an organization

Reference Group

Reference groups are one type of group in an organization. It refers the members who act as a reference for individuals and formed a group on the basis of reference individual from outside of an organization and frame personality by reference members of a team

These groups reference groups have directly or indirectly affected the individual's attitude who are either belonging to a member or not members in an organization

Small Group

It consists of two to five. It is highly effective in the process of decision making in an organization, group members are limited. Communication is very fast among the members of the group in an organization. This type of grouping will take very speed decisions in an organization

Friendship Group
It is one type of group in an organization. It is formed by friends who are in working in an organization. These groups are formed only meet the needs of like belongings and security in an organization.

Task Group
Task groups are one type of group in an organization. It is only concentrated on the task of an organization.
These type of groups are ready take decisions for achievement of the major tasks in an organization.

Self-Managed Group
Self-managed group are one type of group in an organization, a group of worker who supervise their own activities and able to monitor self and produce the quality of the goods and service and it meet ultimate goals of the client.

These groups set own goals and task, for this purpose formed this type group outside of an organization.

Self-Directed Group
It is one type of group in an organization These Group members are working together in an organization and they are self-directed towards the common goal that define discipline, compensation and how to achievement of task in an organization.

Virtual Group
Virtual Team is one type team. This team member rarely or never meet face to face and interact but they are using various forms of information technology such as email, computer networks, telephone, fax and video conferences.

ADVANTAGES OF GROUP DECISIONS
Group decisions have certain advantages over individual decisions.
It Provides more complete information.
Generates the more alternatives.
Increases acceptance of a solution.
Increases legitimacy.
Time consuming.
Minority domination.
Pressures to conform, which can lead to group thinking level. And ambiguous responsibility.

EFFECTIVENESS AND EFFICIENCY OF GROUP DECISION MAKING

It depends on the following criteria used for defining effectiveness:

Group decisions tend to be more accurate.

Individual decisions are quicker in terms of speed.

Group decisions tend to have more acceptances. The effectiveness of group decisions tends to be influenced by the size of the group. Groups Should not be too large. Groups also are not as efficient as individual decision makers.

TECHNIQUES FOR IMPROVING GROUP DECISION MAKING

Brainstorming is an idea-generating process that encourages alternatives while withholding criticism.

Nominal group technique is a group decision-making technique in which group members are physically present but operate independently.

CHAPTER 7

MANAGING THE EFFECTIVE TEAMS

INTRODUCTION
Work teams are formal groups, created by interdependent individuals, who's responsible for attaining goals. Most of us are probably familiar with the concept of a team. However, we may not be as familiar with work teams. All work teams are groups, but only formal groups can be work teams.

There are different types of teams. Four characteristics can be used to distinguish different types of teams.
Teams can vary in their purpose or goal.

The duration of a team tends to be either permanent or temporary.

Team members can be either functional or cross-functional.

Finally, teams can either be supervised or self-managed.

Given these four characteristics, some of the most popular types of teams used today include the following:

A functional team is a type of work team that is composed of a manager and his or her subordinates from a particular functional area.

A self-directed or self-managed team is one that operates without a manager and is responsible for a complete work process or segment that delivers a product or service to an external or internal customer.

A virtual team is one that uses computer technology to link physically dispersed members in order to achieve a common goal.

Finally, a cross-functional team is one in which individuals who are experts in various specialties (or functions) work together on various organizational tasks.

DEVELOPING AND MANAGING EFFECTIVE TEAMS

Teams aren't automatically performing the task at high levels. We need to look more closely at how managers can develop and manage effective teams.

There are eight characteristics associated with effective teams.
Clear goals
Relevant skills
Mutual trust
Unified commitment
Good communication
Negotiating skills
Appropriate leadership
Internal and external support

WHAT'S THINGS INVOLVED WITH MANAGING TEAMS?

In planning, it's important that teams have clear goals and that these goals be clear to and accepted by every member of the team.

Organizing tasks that associated with team and managing a team include clarification of authority and structural issues.

Leading issues include such things as determining what role the leader will play, how conflict will be handled, and what the best communication process is utilized.

Two important controlling issues include how to evaluate the team's performance and how to reward team members

One popular approach is the group incentive plans, it is gain-sharing, which is a program that shares the gains of the efforts of group members with those group members.

In conclusion, a TEAM is a temporary or ongoing task group whose members are charged the working together to identify problems, form a consensus about what should be done, and implement necessary actions in relation to a particular task or organizational area.

TEAMS DIFFER FROM TASK FORCES IN TWO WAYS.
Teams identify problems rather than merely reacting to problems identified by others.
Teams decide the course of action and implement it, rather than leaving the implementation to others.

Teams are widely used today and are often, but not always, task groups from across command groups.

An entrepreneurial team is a group of individuals who have diverse expertise and Come from different backgrounds. So that,

Management bring together and trained and able to develop and implement innovative ideas aimed at creating new products or services or significantly improving existing ones.

Self-managed teams, or autonomous work groups, are working groups given responsibility for a task area without day-to-day supervision and with authority to influence and control both group membership and behavior.
Assessment of the situation is critical in that self-managing teams are not successful in all situations.

Group makeup and proper allocation of needed resources is important.
Team training and guidance in cultivating appropriate norms are important.

Managers need to remove performance obstacles and assistance to help the group continue to learn.

www.ingramcontent.com/pod-product-compliance
Lightning Source LLC
Chambersburg PA
CBHW031533210526
45464CB00014B/2486